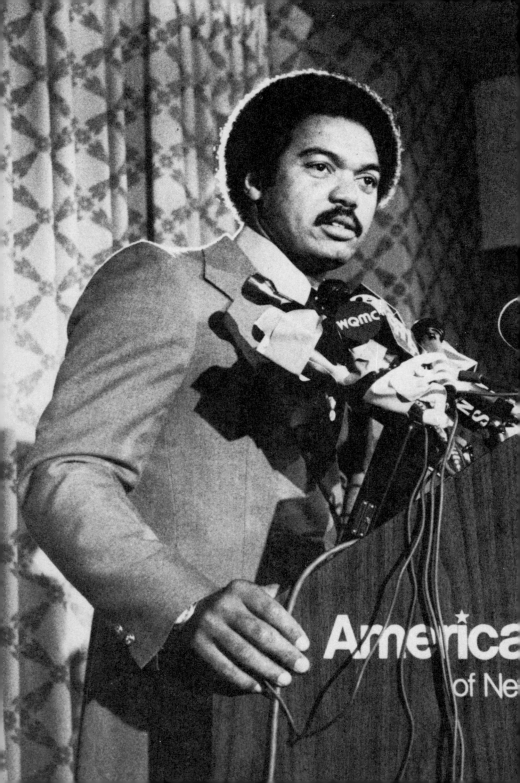

REGGIE JACKSON
The Three Million Dollar Man

BY MAURY ALLEN

photographs (except where noted) by
Louis Requena

Harvey House, Publishers
New York, New York

Cover photograph by Louis Requena

Manufactured in the United States of America
ISBN 0-8178-5817-2

Harvey House, Publishers
20 Waterside Plaza, New York, New York 10010

For Janet, Jennifer and Teddy: My three million dollar people.

Chapter One

There was a feeling of electricity in the air at Yankee Stadium. More than 56,000 people leaned forward in their seats. They were about to witness baseball history. The strong figure in the Yankee uniform, with the large number 44 on his back, pumped his bat out toward the pitcher's mound.

This was the sixth game of the 1977 World Series. The New York Yankees led the Los Angeles Dodgers three games to two. One more New York victory and the World Series would belong to the Yankees for the first time in 15 years. The outcome of the game was hardly in doubt with the Yankees ahead 7-3 in the eighth inning. Most people were concerned more with the next at bat of Reggie Jackson than they were with the final score.

Jackson had hit a home run in his last at-bat two days earlier in Los Angeles. He had walked in his first appearance at the plate on this night, October 18, 1977. Then he had hit a home run on the first pitch to him in the fourth inning. Then he had hit another home run on the first pitch to him in the fifth inning. Now, in the eighth inning, in his final at bat of the season, was it possible he could make history with one swing?

No player had ever hit four home runs in four official at-bats in a World Series game. No player had ever hit

Chris Chambliss, Yankee first baseman, greets Reggie after home run in fifth inning of final game of the 1977 World Series.

three home runs in three swings in one World Series game. Only the great Babe Ruth, the best player in the history of baseball, had ever hit three home runs in a single World Series game.

Now the Dodger pitcher, a big right hander by the name of Charlie Hough, stared down at the sign given by catcher Steve Yeager. Yeager wiggled his three fingers for the familiar pitch. He wanted Hough to throw his best pitch, a knuckleball, which he hoped would whirl and fall under Jackson's lunging swing.

"I guessed knuckleball," Reggie would tell reporters later. "I knew he had to throw his best pitch. I knew I wanted to hit it far. I knew I had never wanted anything in my life as much as I wanted this home run."

Hough stood on the pitching rubber, bent low, lifted

8

his arms high, kicked his left leg toward the plate and threw the ball home. Jackson gripped his fingers tightly against the handle of the bat, peered out from behind his glasses and studied the flight of the baseball.

It was almost on him now, twisting and turning. He swung full and drove the bat at the ball. Crack! The noise could be heard throughout the huge ball park. It sailed onward and upward, racing like a rocket through the night air, crashing hard against the empty section of concrete stands in the deepest part of right center field.

"He did it," screamed a reporter in the press box. "He hit three in three swings. He made history."

Reggie making history with one swing! Dodger catcher Steve Yeager and 56,000 people in Yankee Stadium look on as Reggie hits his fourth World Series home run in four swings.

Soon Jackson was jogging around the bases, his hands held high above his head, his feet lightly dancing on the base paths, his eyes filling with tears, his heart thumping as he neared home plate. He leaped with two feet on the plate and waved to the fans around the Yankee dugout. He tipped his cap, accepted the warm handshakes of his teammates and jumped into the dugout. The noise in the ball park grew and grew and grew into a deafening roar. Jackson stepped on the field again. He blew kisses to the fans and waved his cap at them. Finally the noise subsided.

In the ninth inning the final Dodger batter of the game popped out. Now the fans raced on to the field and Jackson raced off. He rushed into the dugout past the surging crowds. The Yankees were World Champions. In the clubhouse reporters gathered around Reggie.

Somebody asked him if he could compare himself now with Babe Ruth.

"Babe Ruth was great," said Reggie. "I was only lucky."

There was one important difference. Babe Ruth had played before there were televised baseball games. No more than 64,000 people in Yankee Stadium could ever see the Babe in any one game. More than 60 million had seen Reggie that night on television!

On that night, October 18, 1977, all of the boyhood dreams of Reggie Jackson seemed to come true. It was a miracle long in the making.

Reggie with his parents at the ceremony announcing his signing with the Yankees.

Chapter Two

Reginald Martinez Jackson was born May 18, 1946 in Wyncote, Pennsylvania. Soon his parents moved to Cheltenham, a wealthy suburb outside of Philadelphia. There were six children in all in the Jackson family, two older brothers, Joe and James, an older sister, Dolores and two younger sisters, Beverly and Tina.

Jackson's mother is black. His father is part black and part Spanish. Reggie's father's family came from different parts of Latin America.

"The neighborhood where I grew up was mostly white. There was very little prejudice. There were a lot of Jewish people in the neighborhood. We all got along well," Reggie said.

There were more problems inside the home than outside. Reggie's mother and father did not get along. There were fights over money. There never was enough. Reggie's father worked as a tailor and later had his own shop.

When Reggie was only four years old his mother and father separated. Soon they were divorced. The boys, Joe, Jim and Reggie stayed with their father. The girls, Dolores, Beverly and Tina, moved to Baltimore with their mother. Reggie's grandmother lived there.

"When I was a little kid my father left very early for

work," remembers Reggie. "He had a small delivery truck. He piled all the clothes in that truck and I helped him."

On school days Mr. Jackson would be out of the house before seven o'clock. He would be in his shop or out making deliveries. Reggie would be awakened by his older brothers.

"I would get up, dress myself, take a stale piece of bread for breakfast and walk a mile to school. Sometimes I wouldn't eat anything for breakfast. Maybe there wasn't a piece of bread. Maybe I just didn't have the time to eat," Reggie said.

Reggie would come home from school, drink a glass of milk and be outside playing ball in the street. He would dream that he was Jackie Robinson or Roy Campanella or Willie Mays or Hank Aaron. He dreamed that someday he could be out there on a Major League field.

"I liked every game, not just baseball," Reggie said. "We used to play stick ball and dodge ball and running bases and every game kids played. We all played together, black kids and white, Jewish kids and Christians, just out there having a good time."

There was no television then so Reggie would play until dark. Then he would come inside, help his brothers clean the house or run some errands to the grocery store. He would listen to the radio, do his homework and read sports books. It would be late at night before the big event of the entire day.

"That would be when my father would come home from the route. He would drive the truck up to the

14

Posing with Reggie at the 1977 All Star game are (left to right) former Brooklyn Dodger pitcher Joe Black, George "Boomer" Scott of the Boston Red Sox, and Henry Aaron, one of Reggie's boyhood idols.

house and we would hear him yelling for us. We would rush out and he would have a package of meat and a bag of potatoes and sometimes some fruit. Once in a while he would give me a quarter and send me down for some ice cream. We never went hungry," he said.

Mr. Jackson would cook the meal. The boys would clean up. Sometimes, even when he was seven or eight or nine years old, Reggie wouldn't be in bed before eleven o'clock at night.

"There were always chores to do around the house," Reggie said. "I was tired a lot of the time. I had to rake the leaves in the spring and fall, take care of the lawn, paint the house, repair the fences. I was a busy kid."

Somehow there was always enough time to play ball. As Reggie got older the ball playing became more important. At 15 years of age he was nearly six feet tall

15

and 175 pounds. He was on the baseball team in spring and the football team in fall.

"I saw that he was more interested in baseball and football than he was in working around the house," said Mr. Jackson. "I'd let him off his chores early to play if he promised to make it up on the weekends. He always did. He was a good boy."

There were many lonely moments for Reggie. He knew nothing of his mother and never saw her. His father was almost always working. Sometimes Reggie was mean and angry. He didn't really know why.

"One day a kid stole my lunch in school. Lunch? It was a box of pretzels. I told the teacher if I didn't get it back I would bust someone," Reggie said.

One of the other boys was smiling. He knew that the teacher wouldn't do anything about the stolen pretzels. Reggie grabbed the boy. He shoved him against a wall.

"Boy, don't you know I might kill you?"

The frightened boy said he was sorry. Reggie let go of his shirt. It wasn't the boy he was mad at. It was his own life. He was just angry at being alone so much of the time while his classmates told stories of going on picnics and having a good time with their parents.

Sometimes Reggie was jealous of the kids who had more money. If he wanted a candy bar or an ice cream cone he had to work to earn it. Some other kids just seemed to have money in their pockets all the time.

"I was a tough kid. I wasn't scared of anybody. This one time I was in a store with my father and saw the candy counter. I knew my dad was broke. I just picked up the candy bar and put it in my pocket. Later my dad saw it. He make me go back to the store and tell the cashier. I was so ashamed. I never did anything like that again," he said.

As he got older and bigger and stronger, Reggie turned more and more to sports. Football was actually his best game.

"I liked the contact," he said. "One time I hit the line and a defensive lineman punched me in the mouth. He broke my tooth. I asked the quarterback to call my play again. This time I ran over the guy and left him in the dirt in pain."

As his high school years drew to a close, Reggie began thinking about his life. He knew he didn't want to drive a truck or work in a dry cleaning store as his father did. He wasn't quite sure what he wanted to do. In his senior year many colleges began writing him letters and visiting him. Schools all over the country attempted to recruit him. Some wanted him for football. Others wanted him for baseball. One school was willing to let him play both sports.

"The school that interested me the most was Arizona State," he said. "They had a wonderful football program. They said I would be a great running back. They also said I could play baseball there. A lot of the other schools didn't want me to play two sports."

Late in August of 1964, Reggie Jackson flew out to Tempe, Arizona to enter Arizona State University on a football and baseball scholarship.

"It was one of the best decisions of my life," said

Reggie after he was selected as the second man in the 1966 baseball draft. A senior at Arizona State University at the time, Reggie was picked by the Kansas City Athletics. (Wide World Photo)

Reggie. "I really loved it out there. I enjoyed the sun and the clear skies. I liked the people and I made many friends at Arizona State."

Soon Reggie was the biggest thing on campus. He was a star on the football team as a freshman. He was the best running back the school had ever had. In baseball he played centerfield and was the best hitter. He fooled around with the basketball team and the track team. He was almost as good as the varsity players in those sports. He didn't know which sport he would concentrate on.

"In my sophomore year at school I hurt my leg. The

football coach shifted me from running back to a defensive halfback. I didn't like that. I wanted to be the star on the team. I wanted to be the glamour guy. There was no glamour playing defense," he said. Reggie knew from that day on that he would be a baseball player. He could star on his own in baseball. All eyes would be on him. Baseball is a team game but it is easy to see what individuals are doing.

Soon his baseball feats were the talk of the town. Baseball scouts began gathering at Tempe for every game Arizona State played. There was a great deal of interest in Reggie. He was hitting huge home runs. Ball teams can't wait to sign strong young men who can do that.

In June of 1966 the Major Leagues held a free agent draft. This meant that all college players could be selected by Major League teams. If a player chose to sign he would leave college and play baseball. If not, he could stay in school and finish his education.

Two teams were very interested in Jackson. Both were bad teams at that time. One was the Kansas City A's, owned by Charles O. Finley. The other was the New York Mets, owned by Mrs. Joan Whitney Payson. The Mets had first choice in the draft.

Instead of picking Reggie Jackson in the draft—considered the best college player in the country—they chose a young catcher named Steve Chilcott. They soon signed him. He was injured often as a minor league player and soon quit baseball.

Then came the turn of the A's. Charles Finley stood up at the meeting of baseball owners, looked around the room and smiled. Then he announced, "The Kansas A's select the rights to Reggie Jackson."

"Finley immediately flew out to Tempe to talk to me. I told him I didn't want to sign. I told him I wanted to finish college. He raised the offer. I kept saying I wasn't interested. He kept raising the offer," Reggie said.

When Finley raised his price to nearly one hundred thousand dollars, Reggie couldn't fight him anymore.

"I'll sign," he said.

Finley pulled a contract from his inside pocket. He pulled a pen from another pocket. Then Reggie signed his name to his first contract.

He was on the way. He was a professional baseball player. The poor kid from outside Philadelphia, the son of a tailor, was now a great Major League prospect.

"I could only think of all the days of being alone and being hungry," Reggie said. "I had made up with my mom by now and I was still close to my dad. It was just a great day for me, for my parents, my brothers and sisters, for all of us."

Finley brought Jackson into Kansas City to meet with the sportswriters. He charmed them with his cool manner. He liked to talk. He wasn't afraid of the press. They loved him for it.

"I can't wait until this kid comes back to the club and we can interview him every day," one veteran sportswriter said.

Soon Reggie Jackson was on his way West to Lewiston, Idaho in the Northwest League. He would begin his professional career some forty days after he turned twenty years old.

Sitting beside Ed Lopat, executive vice president of the A's, Reggie signs a contract for $85,000. (Wide World Photo)

"I wasn't afraid," he said. "I knew I could handle it. College ball in Arizona State was probably tougher than that league."

While at college Reggie had married his school sweetheart. They soon had a daughter. The marriage wasn't working well. As Reggie took off for professional baseball he knew his marriage was over.

"I was probably too young to get married," he said. "I look back now and I realize I wasn't ready. I just didn't have the maturity to handle it."

He did have the maturity to handle professional baseball. He played in only 12 games for Lewiston before the A's knew they had made a mistake. Reggie was too good for that league. He hit .292, had 11 runs batted in for 12 games and hit two home runs, one over 450 feet from home plate.

"They still talk about the time Reggie played here," said an old sportswriter from Lewiston. "He was a fine player and a fine young man."

The next stop for Reggie Jackson was Modesto, California. He loved the city. There were so many things he had never seen before. The skies were clear blue. The temperatures were mild. It was all a plush dream world after so many years of cold Philadelphia streets and the blazing desert of Arizona.

Jackson batted .299 in 56 games at Modesto. He had 60 runs batted in and crashed 21 home runs, an incredible total in only 221 times at bat. He was the best defensive outfielder in the league and his throwing arm was feared by all runners.

In Kansas City owner Charles O. Finley sat in his offices and asked his assistant, "Should we bring him up now?"

His assistant knew that Finley was talking about only one player, Reggie Jackson.

"I don't think any kid can be ready to play in the Major Leagues after one season in the minors, Mr. Finley," the assistant said.

"Just remember," said Finley, "this isn't any kid. This is Reggie Jackson."

Finley knew that Jackson was going to be a special player. It wasn't that Jackson was big and strong and hit home runs. That was important. It was also that he had personality. He could charm the sportswriters. He could help sell tickets for the A's.

"A player has to be colorful to draw fans," Finley said. "Some players have that. Some players don't. I was always looking for players who did. If they didn't have colorful personalities I invented it for them."

One of the best examples of that came in the signing of a young pitcher in 1964 by the name of Jimmy Hunter. Finley didn't think the name had a colorful ring.

"What do your folks call you?" he asked Hunter, in 1964 when he signed him.

"Jimmy," said the young pitcher.

"And your friends?"

"Jimmy," said the pitcher.

"And what do you like to do when you're not playing baseball?"

"Go huntin' and fishin' all of the time."

"What do you catch?"

"Catfish," said the pitcher.

"We'll call you Catfish," said Finley.

Four former A's gather before a game at Yankee Stadium in 1977. From left to right are Ken Holtzman, pitcher, Reggie, Joe Rudi, outfielder now with the California Angels, and pitcher Jim "Catfish" Hunter.

So Jim Hunter became Catfish Hunter. Reginald Martinez Jackson was always Reggie. He would stay that way. It was a colorful name.

In 1967 the A's were signing many young players. They were building a fine team for the future. Their best players were being sent to their Birmingham, Alabama farm club.

On April 16, 1967 Reggie Jackson opened up his first full season of professional ball in Birmingham. His long home runs, his speed, his great arm, his marvelous defensive ability made him a quick star in the Alabama city. Something else was going on in Birmingham at the time.

"It was the height of the civil rights movement," he said. "There were a lot of angry people in town. I had to show them by playing ball that I was the equal of any white player."

With the pressure to excel he started slowly. Soon his bat came alive. He was hitting huge home runs all over the Southern Association parks. By mid-season Reggie Jackson was the talk of the league. By late summer sportswriters in Birmingham were calling Jackson the best player to ever play in the league. He was called up to the A's late in August but not before he batted .293 for Birmingham, hit 17 home runs and had 58 runs batted in. He was a unanimous choice of sportswriters around the league as the PLAYER OF THE YEAR.

"It was a great honor," Reggie said. "It was very important to me because of the times we were living in. I wanted to impress the A's but I wanted most to impress the people in Birmingham."

Chapter Three

Soon Jackson was in the big leagues with Kansas City. He was staying in modern hotels and eating in the finest restaurants while he visited cities he had only dreamed of seeing when he was back in Philadelphia. As the saying goes, "it was all happening" for Reggie.

"Maybe it was all happening too fast," said Reggie. "I couldn't deal with it. For the first time in my life I wasn't the star of my team. This was the big leagues. Everybody was a star here."

The big league pitchers were showing the kid some new tricks. He hadn't seen any of these pitches in Arizona State or in the minors. He was puzzled.

"I doubted my ability. For the first time I worried if I was good enough," he said.

"We never doubted it for one minute," said Finley. "Once you see Reggie swing a bat you know he belongs in the big leagues."

All through the winter of 1967-1968 there were rumors about Finley's team. He was unhappy in Kansas City and the people of Kansas City were unhappy with him. The team was young and inexperienced. The fans were tired of watching the A's lose. Finley decided to move his team to Oakland.

Before the move was completed Finley lined up one man to help him. That man was Joe DiMaggio, the retired Hall of Famer of the New York Yankees. DiMaggio had been out of baseball since 1951 but Finley talked him into helping out the A's in Oakland. DiMaggio lived in nearby San Francisco.

"I went to spring training and worked with the young players," DiMaggio said. "One of the best young players I saw was Reggie Jackson."

"It was just a great thrill for me," said Jackson. "When I was a kid DiMaggio had already finished his career. He was still a name everybody knew: The Yankee Clipper. We all wanted to be as good as he was."

Day after day, under the hot sun in the Arizona training camp of the A's, DiMaggio worked with Jackson.

"He had all the tools," DiMaggio said. "My job was to teach him how to use them. You can't teach a young fellow how to run or throw or hit with power. But if he can do those things you can teach him how to take advantage of his skills."

There were so many things to learn. Reggie had to study the pitchers. He had to know what pitch he would most likely get in a specific situation. He had to learn when he could pull and when he should hit straight away. It was harder than anything he ever had to deal with at college.

"I would go to sleep at night and my head would be spinning," Reggie said. "There were so many things to remember. I hoped I could keep them all in my head."

The A's left Arizona for their first game in Oakland. DiMaggio got a big cheer from his fans in the Bay area. All the A's got big cheers. One of the biggest cheers

Reggie shows his batting stance in 1968.

greeted the announcement that Reggie Jackson would start in right field for Oakland. He was already a crowd favorite even before he had played a single game there.

Manager Bob Kennedy put the rookie in right field and left him there. If he had a bad day he would ask to have DiMaggio work with him a little extra. If Reggie had a good day he would just glow. The press in Oakland quickly found Reggie to be interesting and honest.

"The sportswriters have a job to do," he said. "I understood that. As long as they wrote it the way I said it was fine with me. I didn't mind the attention. I liked it."

Jackson had one major problem as a rookie. He was striking out too much. It didn't bother him as much as it did manager Bob Kennedy.

"He has to learn how to make more contact," said Kennedy.

"I can't cut down on my swing," said Reggie. "That's what got me here. All sluggers strike out. Babe Ruth set the record."

Jackson wasn't comparing himself to the Babe. He was just making a point. If a player was going to hit a lot of home runs he had to swing hard. Nobody in baseball swung harder than Reggie Jackson.

The A's were not going anywhere in 1968. Jackson concentrated on his own hitting. The strikeouts cost some games but they excited the crowd. When the season ended Reggie had batted only .250. But he had socked 29 home runs and had 74 runs batted in. He also struck out 171 times to lead the league.

All around the league they were talking about Jackson. His power was attracting a great deal of attention.

"If anybody is going to break Roger Maris' home run record," said New York Yankee manager Ralph Houk, "it might be that kid Jackson."

Roger Maris had hit 61 homers in 1961. The Babe had hit 60 in 1927. Now Maris had the new record. Jackson was nominated as a candidate to top him.

"I'm young, I'm strong, anything is possible," said Jackson. "I'm not going for it but it could happen."

It almost happened in 1969. Reggie got off to a wonderful start on the season. By early June he was ahead of the record pace of Maris. He might break the record. Stories filled the papers every day about Reggie.

"The pressure was great," Reggie remembers. "I just wasn't ready for it."

At the middle of the season, play stopped for a few days for the All-Star game. That year it was held in Washington, D.C. A banquet was held in The White House for all the players and press.

President Richard Nixon greeted all the players. One by one, they walked in a line and were introduced to the President. The President would say a few words to each of the players.

"I'm glad to meet you, Reggie," the President told Jackson. "I've been following your career. I'll be rooting for you to get that record."

"Thank you, Mr. President," Reggie said.

Reggie could not help but think how far he had come—a poor tailor's son from Philadelphia—having

Reggie with slugging first baseman, Mike Epstein.

the President of the United States greet him in The White House.

Sportswriters were very interested in asking Reggie if he thought he had a chance to break the record of Maris. He was happy to talk about it.

"If I stay healthy," he said, "I think I have a good chance."

Unfortunately, he didn't stay healthy. He suffered shoulder and back injuries. He caught a bad cold. He lost weight and grew weak as the season went on.

"As the season went on," Reggie remembers, "the pressure became too much. I was too young for that kind of attention. If I was older I might have been able to do it."

At 23 years old Reggie just couldn't deal with all the attention and all the talk. He began to avoid the press. It was not like him.

He had a large slump in September. He not only didn't hit 61 home runs to tie Roger Maris, he didn't even win the home run title. Harmon Killebrew of the Minnesota Twins hit 49. Reggie ended up with 47 homers, 118 runs batted in, an average of .275 and only 142 strikeouts.

"You could see him mature that year as a player," said the new Oakland manager, Hank Bauer. "It would have been a wonderful year if the press didn't make a fuss about the home run record. After all, how many players ever hit 47?"

Jackson went to spring training in 1970 with high hopes. He was coming off that wonderful year. Finley was working hard and spending money to improve the A's. There was hope in Oakland that the team would be ready to challenge for the top spot. The A's had finished second in 1969. A new manager, John McNamara, was now in charge of the team.

"We had a young club that was just about ready to develop," McNamara said. "I think we could have won the pennant. Reggie just didn't have a very good year."

Reggie Jackson doesn't like to think about 1970. It probably was the unhappiest year he ever had in the Major Leagues. His batting average dropped to .237. He hit only 23 home runs. He had only 66 runs batted in. He still struck out 135 times.

"There was so much expected of me. I put too much pressure on myself. I thought I could break the home run record. I thought I would lift my average. I thought we would win the pennant," he said.

When the season was over Reggie Jackson went back to Arizona. He was very unhappy. He didn't enjoy playing baseball. He even considered quitting. He thought maybe he could go into the real estate business full time. It was probably the low point of his life.

"I had a lot of good friends. I talked over my problems with them. They convinced me I was still a great player. They told me I had to relax. They proved to me that friends are the most important thing in the world when you are down," Reggie said.

In 1971 the baseball world waited to see if Reggie Jackson would make a comeback. He was still very young, only twenty-four when the season started, and had time to improve. He worked hard in spring training. He stayed out long after his teammates had gone in for the day. He took batting practice until the skin on his hands bled. He took extra sliding practice until his thighs were raw. He worked on every aspect of his game. He wanted to be a complete player.

The A's had their fourth manager in four years. This time they had a winner. Charles Finley hired Dick Williams as field boss. Williams had managed the Red Sox to the pennant in 1967.

"I saw all that talent in Reggie immediately," said Williams. "The only thing that could prevent Reggie from being a great star was Reggie himself. I didn't think that could happen."

All of the young players on the A's were about ready to star in the Major Leagues. They had some great players including Sal Bando, Dick Green, Bert Campaneris, Catfish Hunter, Joe Rudi and Vida Blue. Reggie was the leader.

"I think if we could have kept all of these players together for several years we would have challenged a lot of the records of the great teams," said Williams.

There were some good players and some strange people playing for the A's. Sometimes their personalities got in the way of their playing. They had arguments on and off the field. Once in a while there were fights. They were known as the Battling A's.

"It's impossible to be together every day for more than six months," said manager Williams, "and not disagree."

Dick Williams had been the manager of the Boston Red Sox in 1967. The Red Sox won the pennant that year. The team had gone from ninth place in 1966 to first place in 1967. Boston was known that year as the "Impossible Dream Team."

"There was a lot of talent on the Oakland team when I came there. I had to help them learn how to play winning baseball. I had to teach them a team philosophy. They had so much ability I knew they could win," he said.

The Oakland A's won their first Western Division championship in 1971. Reggie had another marvelous year. He batted .277 in 150 games, hit 32 home runs and batted in 80 runs.

"I matured as a player," Reggie said. "I learned more about baseball in that one season than I had learned in all the years I had played before."

Williams saw that Reggie would be an excellent player, a team leader, if he could learn to handle himself.

"He's an emotional player. He could get very high-strung. The idea was to teach him to control himself on the field. He soon learned it," Williams said.

The mark of a true champion is how well he performs under pressure. A lot of ball players can do well during the season. Only the great ones do well in the championship play in the post-season. Jackson showed what he was made of in his first playoff.

On October 3, 1971 Reggie Jackson took the field in Baltimore against the Orioles in the first playoff game of his life. His mother was in the stands. His father had come down from Philadelphia. He had purchased some 25 tickets for his sisters and brothers, uncles and aunts, nieces and nephews.

"Maybe that is why I was so nervous when the game started. I had so many people out there I wanted to do well for," he said. "It's always a little tougher playing for your family."

After the first at bat and the first outfield catch, Reggie settled down. He played very well. He had a hit in each game, played fine defensive baseball, smashed two home runs and was the Oakland star. Unfortunately, the Orioles won three games straight and the championship series.

"We couldn't handle the pressure," Reggie said. "Suddenly you look around and the park is filled. Suddenly you see more newspaper reporters and more television cameramen than you knew ever existed. It was too much."

Another home run for Jackson.

After the playoffs ended Reggie went back to his home in Arizona. He rested, he involved himself in the real estate business, he thought over all the things that had happened in 1971.

"Maybe we weren't ready mentally," He told Garry Walker, his business partner and friend. "Maybe there were too many other things on my mind."

Reggie made a vow to himself. When the A's got into the playoffs the next season—and he was sure they would—he would be better prepared. He would close out his mind to all thoughts but one: winning.

Chapter Four

There was one more matter of business left before Reggie could begin the 1972 season with a clear head. He had to sign a contract to play for the A's.

Charles O. Finley, the owner of the team, was a very tough man to deal with. Finley tried to keep the salaries of all his players down. He claimed that his team played in a small park before small crowds. He couldn't afford the salaries that some of the other stars in the league were making.

"I knew what I was worth," said Reggie. "If he couldn't afford to pay me he could trade me."

There were many letters exchanged between Reggie and Finley. There were numerous phone calls. There were telegrams. Still, no progress. Reggie said he wouldn't play unless his price was met. Finley said he couldn't pay Reggie what he wanted.

Almost all of Finley's players wanted more money. Even more than Reggie, Vida Blue was angry. Blue was the best young pitcher in baseball. He had won 24 games in 1971. He had excited fans all across the country. He had drawn capacity crowds in every park he performed in. He had been paid $20,000 for the 1971 season. He wanted more than $50,000 for 1972.

"Never," shouted Finley.

"I'll quit," said Blue.

They argued many times. Finally Blue announced that he was indeed quitting baseball at 22 years old. A week later he showed up as a vice-president for a plumbing supply company.

"That dude really means it," said Reggie.

Finally Reggie agreed to terms. He would be paid $75,000 for the 1972 season. Blue continued to hold out. Reggie called him on the phone.

"I'm with you," he said.

Shortly before the season began Blue signed his contract for $40,000. The battle was over.

"I thought baseball was a sport," said Blue. "I learned it was a hard business."

The contract struggle hurt Blue badly. He didn't pitch well in 1972. He won only six games and lost ten. Reggie understood what he was going through.

"It takes a while to understand the mental aspects of the game," said Jackson. "Vida was shocked by Charlie's greed. I think sooner or later we all have to grow up. I know Vida grew up after negotiating with Charlie."

Even with Blue having a bad year the A's played well. Catfish Hunter won 21 games. Ken Holtzman won 19 games. Rollie Fingers was an excellent relief pitcher. The A's won their second straight division title.

Reggie had batted .265 with 25 home runs and 75 runs batted in. More importantly, he had been an excellent team player all year. Now it was on to Detroit for the league championship against the Tigers.

"As I sat in my hotel room the night before the first game," said Reggie, "I realized what the game was all about. We had won the division but we hadn't won the pennant. I knew we all had to play hard to win. I vowed I would play harder than I had ever played in my life."

Jackson lived up to his vow. It all came down to the final playoff game, Thursday, October 12, 1972 in Detroit. The Tigers and the A's were tied at two games each. The winner of the game would win the American League pennant.

Detroit quickly took a one run lead in the first inning. In the second with one out Jackson singled and went to third on a single by Mike Epstein. Then manager Dick Williams signaled for a double steal.

Jackson broke for home plate. The throw went to second baseman Tony Taylor of the Tigers. He quickly threw the ball home as hard as he could. There was a sickening crash at home plate as Jackson ran into Detroit catcher Bill Freehan.

The pain rushed through Reggie's body. He broke into a violent sweat. His body was shaking from the collision. He looked up at umpire Nestor Chylak. "Was I safe?" he asked. Chylak had already signaled that he was but Reggie couldn't see it from his position. "That's good," he said.

The Oakland trainer was on the field. He examined Reggie's leg. Nothing was broken but Reggie had severely torn the upper right hamstring. He would not be able to walk without crutches for several weeks.

When the World Series opened up in Cincinnati two

days later, Reggie was on the bench in street clothes. He needed crutches to get from one end of the dugout to the other. He stayed there every game. He rooted for his teammates as they defeated Cincinnati to become champions of the world.

"I cried when it was over," Reggie said. "I had worked all my life to get into the World Series. When my team finally made it I was on crutches."

On crutches, Reggie joins the A's as they are introduced at the beginning of the 1972 World Series. On Jackson's right is manager Dick Williams. Reggie received permission to sit on the A's bench in civilian clothes for the series. (Wide World Photo)

*Reggie sits this one out while Yankees Chris Chambliss (#10),
Thurman Munson (#15) and Manager Bill Virdon (#21) argue
with the umpire.*

Chapter Five

The A's were again favored to win the pennant as the team began spring training in 1973. Owner Charles O. Finley had built a marvelous team. There seemed little question the A's had the talent to win again. The most serious question about the A's was: Could they get along?

"There were a lot of strong personalities on that team," said pitcher Ken Holtzman. "You never knew what player would explode."

Reggie ran hard and hit well in spring training. His leg was normal. So was his mouth. He told sportswriters the A's would win again and he predicted he would have a great season.

A lot of his teammates thought Reggie talked too much. A lot of them didn't like the way he hung around with sportswriters and got so much attention. A lot of his teammates thought he did things for show on the field. They thought he was more concerned with drawing attention to himself than he was about whether the team was winning. In baseball such a player is called a hot dog.

Sportswriters would often go to other players on the team to ask their opinions of Reggie. Some of them were jealous. Some paid little attention to him. A pitcher by the name of Darold Knowles probably said it best. He was asked one day what he thought of his teammate Reggie Jackson.

"Reggie is such a hot dog," he said, "there isn't enough mustard in all America to cover him."

Reggie took most of the kidding well. He never seemed to get angry about it. He loved the attention. He knew he had a big ego.

"I think it doesn't matter what you say in the game," Reggie once said, "as long as you play well."

How well he played in 1973!

He was 27 years old that May. He had been in the big leagues for six full seasons. He had learned the game well. He had arrived as a star and he excelled in 1973 with his finest season. He was no longer a star. Now he was a superstar.

Jackson led the league in home runs with 32. He batted in 117 runs. His average was .293. He led the league in runs scored with 99. He had his picture on the cover of many national magazines and was one of the few baseball players to ever have his picture on the cover of *Time*.

"You can't imagine what a thrill this is," he said.

The A's won the division championship again, beat Baltimore again for the American League pennant and faced the New York Mets in the World Series.

Many of the largest newspapers, wire services, magazines and television stations are in New York. A baseball player who does well in New York gets more attention.

"It's more important to do well playing in New York or against a New York team than against anybody else," Reggie said.

Somebody asked Reggie before the World Series began if he would like to play for a New York team.

"If I played in New York," he said, "they would name a candy bar after me."

A candy bar called *Baby Ruth* had become associated with Babe Ruth even though it had actually been named after President Grover Cleveland's daughter, Ruth. Another candy bar, *Oh Henry,* had become associated with Henry Aaron.

"If I get to New York I'm sure they will make a Reggie bar in my honor," he said.

The World Series began in Oakland. Owner Charles O. Finley sat in his front row box seat. There was a telephone next to his seat. Before the first pitch he picked up the phone. A few minutes later a press box runner made an announcement from Finley. "I just phoned President Nixon in Washington. I asked him to throw out the first ball tomorrow. He said he couldn't come. But he was watching the game."

The Series was very hard fought. It was all tied up three games each after six games. The championship would be settled in the final game on October 21, 1973. The starting pitchers were Ken Holtzman for Oakland and Jon Matlack for the Mets.

Holtzman doubled in the third inning and shortstop Bert Campaneris hit a home run for a 2-0 Oakland lead.

Then Joe Rudi singled to center. Sal Bando popped out. Jackson was up.

"I had watched Matlack closely," said Jackson. "I knew how he tried to pitch me. I knew he would throw a fastball high and inside. I was ready for it."

The pitch came in exactly where Jackson expected and he was ready for it. He swung hard and connected with all of his might.

"There is such a sweet feeling when you hit a ball that good," he said. "You can feel the excitement all through your body."

The ball crashed into the seats some 450 feet from home plate. The Oakland fans went wild. The A's now led 4-0. They knew that the A's would win again. Soon the game was over. The A's were champs for the second time in a row.

"Only the great teams ever win the World Series two years in a row," said Jackson. "I'm proud we could do it. Now that we have won twice I want to win three times in a row, then four, then five, then six. Nobody has ever won six."

The New York Yankees, under manager Casey Stengel, had won the World Series five years in a row from 1949-1953. No other baseball team had ever come close.

Reggie went back home to Arizona. He felt wonderful. He knew this had been his finest season. Only one more thing remained to make it perfect. The Baseball Writers Association of America would soon name the Most Valuable Player in the American League.

In the first week of November they made the announcement. Reggie Jackson had been named the MVP of the American League in a landslide vote. He was now generally considered one of the best players in the game.

"I accept this award on behalf of all my teammates," he said.

Reggie in action during 1973 World Series against the New York Mets. (Left) Joe Rudi congratulates Jackson after home run. (Right) Reggie makes catch in right field as A's center fielder Bill North backs up the play.

Chapter Six

Once again Reggie struggled with owner Charles O. Finley over his salary. Finley would not pay Reggie what the outfielder thought he was worth after his MVP season.

"Everybody in baseball recognizes me as a superstar," said Reggie, "except the man who pays me."

They finally came to terms for $100,000 for the 1974 season and Reggie reported to camp. He had one aim in the spring of 1974. He wanted to help the A's win again.

"The only teams to ever win three championships in a row were the Yankees. I want to be classed with them," he said.

The A's were able to do it. Oakland won the division title, beat Baltimore again and defeated the Los Angeles Dodgers in the 1974 World Series. Now they were in the same class with the Yankees.

Baseball was changing in 1975. For more than a century, all baseball players had been tied to their teams by a condition in their contract called the reserve clause. It meant that players could not offer their services to any club other than the club that owned them.

Many players felt this reserve clause was unfair. One player, Curt Flood, had taken his case to court. He was represented by former Supreme Court Justice Arthur Goldberg. Flood lost the case. The reserve clause still stood.

The bench of the "Battling A's." Reggie is capless, standing in the front.

The players had a union. It was called the Major League Baseball Players Association and was headed by Marvin Miller. This association bargained for the rights of players. The association negotiated with the owners of the teams. One day, after long bargaining, the owners agreed to salary arbitration. This meant that players could argue for higher salaries before an arbitration board. If members of the Oakland A's no longer liked the salary they were offered by Finley, they could present their cases to impartial arbitration. Many did. Many won higher salaries. A few players lost.

Jackson had another good year in 1975. He led the league with 36 homers. He had 104 runs batted in. He batted .253. This time the A's won the division title but lost the league championship to Boston.

"The great team that we had for years was breaking up," said Jackson. "So many players were so angry at Finley you could feel it in the clubhouse."

There were more disputes among the players. One day outfielder Billy North and Jackson got into a fight. They began punching each other in the clubhouse. Then they wrestled on the floor as many players just watched.

47

Only one player, catcher Ray Fosse, did anything. He suffered a pulled muscle in his shoulder trying to break up the fight.

"I was sitting there playing cards," Ken Holtzman said. "I never even looked at the fight. After all, this was the clubhouse of the Oakland A's. Only one bad thing happened during the fight. I didn't concentrate on my cards and lost the hand."

Finley could see that his players were unhappy. He knew they wanted more money than he could afford to pay. He realized he had to trade them and get players who would play for less money. On April 2, 1976 he surprised the baseball world by trading Reggie Jackson to Baltimore.

"I was shocked," said Reggie. "I had played my entire career with the A's. I wasn't consulted. I was traded to Baltimore like a slab of meat."

Jackson announced that he would quit baseball. He stayed home in Arizona and concentrated on the real estate business. The Orioles opened their season without him.

In the meantime the Major League Players Association continued to negotiate with the owners. They came to an agreement. It provided that players could leave their teams if they didn't sign a contract and sign with another team. They would be called free agents, free to sell their services to the highest bidder. Ball players were no longer bound to a team for life.

"I decided to report to the Orioles," Jackson said. "I hoped I could get a contract there. My mother lived in Baltimore. I was glad she could see me play."

Scenes from Reggie's year with the Baltimore Orioles. (Top left) Al Bumbry greets Jackson after two-run homer. (Top right) Jackson takes right field against the Yankees. (Bottom) Always a favorite with the fans, Reggie signs autographs before a game.

Throughout the 1976 season Jackson played well. He batted .277 for Baltimore, hit 27 home runs and knocked in 91 runs. The Orioles tried to sign him, but he refused. He felt he could make more money with another team.

On November 2, 1976 baseball owners met in the grand ballroom of the Plaza Hotel in New York City. This was the site of the first free agent reentry draft. This meant teams could pick players who were free agents and try to sign them.

All the teams were called and announced the names of the players they hoped to sign. Now it was the turn of the Yankees. President Gabe Paul of the Yankees moved to the microphone.

"The New York Yankees select the rights to Reggie Jackson," he said.

Now it was all possible. The Yankees might sign him. The most glamorous player in the game may wind up playing for the most glamorous team in baseball history. The Yankees of Babe Ruth, Joe DiMaggio, Lou Gehrig and Mickey Mantle might also be the Yankees of Reggie Jackson.

Could the Yankees sign him? Would he like New York? Would New York like him? Would somebody actually name a candy bar after him if he played in New York?

Several other teams wanted to sign Reggie. There would be a stiff competition. Teams would call the office of Reggie's agent and friend, Garry Walker, with new offers. The price began to go up and up and up. Montreal wanted to sign him very badly as did San Diego. The Yankees were determined to sign him.

50

"I felt that Reggie not only would be a great player but he would be great for New York," said Yankee owner George Steinbrenner.

The figures reached two million dollars. Then two and a half million. Then nearly three million dollars. Some teams offered Reggie more than three million dollars if he would sign with them for the next five seasons.

On a Tuesday afternoon George Steinbrenner flew by private plane to Chicago. Reggie was meeting with several owners there. Steinbrenner told Reggie he wanted to make him a new offer.

"Have lunch with me on Thursday," Steinbrenner said.

"Certainly," said Reggie.

Reggie flew back to New York. Steinbrenner sent a car out to the airport to meet him. They had lunch at the Plaza Hotel in the Palm Court. Then they walked out in to the street together.

A small black boy, about eight years old, spotted Reggie walking with Steinbrenner.

"Reggie, Reggie," he yelled, "sign this please."

The boy pulled a piece of paper from out of his school notebook. Reggie asked his name then signed a personal note.

"I love you, Reggie," the boy said. "Please play in New York."

Steinbrenner reminded Reggie how much the people of New York, especially the kids, wanted him to play in the new Yankee Stadium as a Yankee.

"I think that kid convinced me," Jackson said.

Chapter Seven

On November 29, 1976, reporters were called to a press conference in the Americana Hotel in New York. The Yankees had a major announcement.

Gabe Paul, Reggie Jackson and George Steinbrenner stood on the platform of the large room. Paul moved to the microphones.

"We are pleased to announce that the New York Yankees have signed Reggie Jackson to a five year contract," Paul said.

Reporters raced out of the room. They called their newspapers. Soon the story was going all over the country. The Yankees had signed Reggie Jackson for five years to a contract worth three million dollars. No baseball player, not Babe Ruth, not Lou Gehrig, not Joe DiMaggio, not Mickey Mantle, had ever been paid as much.

Reggie Jackson was the Yankees' Three Million Dollar Man.

"I know there will be a lot of pressure on me," Reggie said. "I can handle it. I always have."

Stories about the Three Million Dollar Man filled the newspapers. Everyone wanted to know how Reggie's large salary would be accepted by his teammates.

"George Steinbrenner promised me I would be the highest paid Yankee. As long as I am, I will be happy," said the Yankee captain, catcher Thurman Munson.

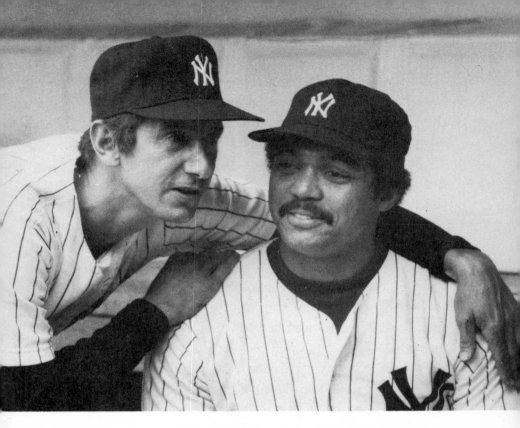

Not fighting for the moment, Yankee Manager Billy Martin has a word with Jackson. From the expression on Reggie's face it is not clear if Billy is giving Reggie advice, encouragement or a warning.

Soon Munson found out he was not the highest paid Yankee. He was very angry and seemed upset all winter. He didn't like what he read or heard about Jackson. He also talked to players on the Oakland A's. A lot of them said they didn't like him. The same complaint about Reggie kept coming up over and over again. He was a hot dog.

The press was all over Reggie as spring training began for the Yankees in Fort Lauderdale, Florida. He gave endless interviews. He did many television interviews.

His picture was in all the papers. The Yankee players grew more and more resentful. The Yankees had won the pennant in 1976 without him. A lot of people wondered if they could win it again in 1977 *with* him.

George Steinbrenner was the owner of the Yankees. Billy Martin was the manager. Reggie was the right fielder. All three men liked attention.

"Is New York big enough for all three?" many people asked.

Martin seemed to go out of his way to be mean to Reggie. He refused to play him in some games. He refused to bat him in the fourth position, the clean-up spot where Reggie had batted for the A's. Often they did not talk.

For several days Thurman Munson, too, refused to talk to Reggie. He walked by him several times without saying a word.

"I was new," said Reggie. "It wasn't my place to greet him. He had to make me welcome."

Reggie gave an interview to a magazine writer. Reggie said he would lead the Yankees. He described his position on the team in colorful terms. He said the Yankees were like a barrel of butter and he was like the churn. He would make them go.

All of this made Reggie unliked by his new teammates. Only one player, catcher Fran Healy, went out of his way to be friendly with Reggie.

"Reggie is a very sensitive man," said Healy. "You have to understand him to like him. He can be very moody, high one day and low the next."

The Yankees opened up the 1977 season. They had

(Left) Losing his glasses and helmet in the process, Jackson comes home. Teammate Graig Nettles (#9) signals Reggie to slide. (Right) Reggie takes a hard swing at the ball but misses.

added Reggie Jackson and pitcher Don Gullett, another high priced free agent, to the team. This club had been good enough to win in 1976. Everybody expected it would win easily in 1977.

It didn't work that way. The entire team was not playing well. Reggie wasn't hitting much. His fielding was terrible. He seemed to have trouble seeing the ball in the outfield. He went for several eye examinations. Reggie wore glasses and the eye doctors said the glasses were fine. There was no need to change.

Soon the magazine article came out. It angered Munson. He said he would never speak to Reggie again. Other players sided with Munson against Reggie. Billy Martin was upset that Jackson failed to play as well as Martin thought he should.

The tension grew. On June 18, 1977, the Yankees were playing in Boston. The game was being seen on national television. A ball was hit to right field. Jackson failed to catch it. Martin thought he did not hustle.

Martin stopped the game and pulled Reggie out. Astonished by Martin's action, Reggie ran bewildered and upset into the Yankee dugout. Martin and Reggie began shouting at each other. Reggie charged toward his manager. Yogi Berra, a former Yankee manager and now a coach, had to hold Reggie back.

"Let me go," screamed Reggie. "I want to kill him."

Martin was being restrained by other Yankee players.

"Let me go," he yelled. "I'll show him who is boss."

The whole episode was seen on national television. Most people thought it was disgusting. Major Leaguers were not supposed to act that way. Owner Steinbrenner called the manager and the player together. He said he wouldn't tolerate any more conduct like that.

"Just tell him to stay away from me," Reggie said.

For a while things grew calm. The Yankees still weren't winning. Boston was in first place during early August. The Yankees had to do something to catch up.

Steinbrenner suggested Martin put Reggie in the fourth spot in the order. Martin resisted. He didn't want anybody to think Steinbrenner was making out the lineup. That was the manager's job.

On August 10, 1977 the Yankees played Oakland at Yankee Stadium. Reggie's name was listed fourth on the lineup card. The Yankees won. Reggie batted in the lead run. The Yankees began winning.

Action from 1977 Yankee season. (Top left) Reggie, in a quiet moment, with Yankee catcher Thurman Munson. (Top right) Jackson stares at Oriole pitcher Jim Palmer after Palmer had thrown a brush-back pitch, knocking Reggie to the ground. (Bottom) After taking a full cut Reggie can't believe the ball ended up in Texas Ranger catcher Jim Sundberg's hand instead of in the right field bleachers.

Reggie holds court with reporters in front of his locker in the Yankee clubhouse.

Chapter Eight

In the last 49 games of the season, after being put in the fourth spot in the lineup, Jackson batted in 50 runs. The Yankees won 40 of those games.

On October 1, 1977 the Yankees clinched the pennant as Boston lost. The players all celebrated in the clubhouse.

"Unless we win it all," said Reggie, "we haven't won anything."

The next stop was the playoffs. In 1976 the Yankees won the pennant on a ninth inning home run by Chris Chambliss in the final playoff game of the season.

Now they were in the final playoff game again. Kansas City led the Yankees 3-1 in the eighth inning. Two more innings and they would be American League champions.

Billy Martin had benched Jackson that day because Paul Splittorff, a fine lefthanded pitcher, was going for Kansas City. Jackson, a strong lefthanded hitter, often had trouble with Splittorff.

"In all the time in Oakland," said teammate Catfish Hunter, "Reggie never hit Splittorff."

So he stayed on the bench. Now Doug Bird, a fine righthanded relief pitcher, was on the mound. The Yankees had two runners on. Cliff Johnson was the scheduled hitter. But wait. . .Reggie was coming off the bench as a pinch hitter.

"I stood at the plate and I was praying for a hit," he said. "I knew all eyes were on me."

The count went to 1-2. Bird threw a fastball. Reggie swung and dropped a single into centerfield. Now the score was 3-2.

In the ninth inning the Yankees made three more runs and won the game 5-3. They were champions of the American League.

"Until we win the World Series we haven't won anything," said Reggie.

The 1977 World Series opened on October 11, 1977 in Yankee Stadium. Reggie was in right field. He was batting fourth against the Los Angeles Dodgers. He got a hit his first time up. The Yankees won the opener 4-3.

The Dodgers won the second game 6-1. The Yankees took the third game of the Series 5-3 with a victory in Los Angeles. Then the Yankees won 4-2. They needed only one more victory. On Sunday, October 16, the Dodgers won 10-4. Reggie Jackson hit a home run his final time at bat.

"I really feel good," he said. "I'm swinging good. I'm looking forward to the next game."

What a next game! No one will ever forget it.

Reggie walked his first time up. Chris Chambliss followed with a home run. Reggie's next time up came in the fourth inning. The pitcher was Burt Hooton for the Dodgers. He was famous for a pitch called the knuckle curve.

"I knew he would throw me that pitch," said Reggie. "I just leaned back and waited for it."

Then he swung. The ball jumped off his bat and went

Reggie on deck with the Yankee batboy during final game of the 1977 World Series.

on a line into the seats in right field. The Yankees led for the first time in the game 4-3.

In the fifth inning Reggie faced a righthander by the name of Elias Sosa. He had seen him only a couple of times before.

"I asked some of the other fellows on the bench about him. Some had played in the National League. They said he would try to keep the ball low on me," Reggie said.

Fans in the right field bleachers hold up "Reggie" signs but Jackson chooses to watch the game instead.

It was low. So was Reggie's bat. The ball flew off the bat and headed again for the right field stands. It landed about ten rows behind his first home run. Reggie Jackson had two home runs in one World Series game.

The Yankees were far in front. They were to win 8-4. All that seemed to matter was Reggie's next at bat. It came in the eighth inning.

"I was nervous as a cat when I went to the plate," said Reggie. "I knew what everybody wanted. I knew what I had to try."

He tried and he succeeded. His final swing of the 1977 season resulted in one of the longest home runs of his career. It was his third of the game. Only Babe Ruth had ever had three home runs in a World Series game.

It was an amazing ending to an incredible season for the Three Million Dollar Man.

Oh yes, one other thing about Reggie Jackson. They finally brought out a candy bar in his honor. Naturally, it was called a *Reggie Bar*.

Reggie surrounded by an assortment of adoring Yankee fans.

About the Author

Maury Allen is a nationally known sportswriter and free lance author. He has more than ten books, 100 articles and thousands of newspaper stories to his credit on all sports. Mr. Allen is the former chairman of the New York Baseball Writers' Association. In 1974 he received an award for the Best Sports Stories. *Reggie Jackson* is Mr. Allen's first book for Harvey House.